The First Time Dog Owner's Guide to a New Puppy

by Shel Gatto

ISBN: 978-1478206125

Special thanks to the Fogle family and their dog Dozer, the Stewart-Bujac family and their dog Liza, the Kosik family and their dog Baeli, the McNally family and their dog Bindi, my good friend Kris Wahler and his dog Phantom, my brother Sean Bollman, my husband Allan and our loving canines for allowing me to include so many wonderful photos in this guide.

Table of Contents

Welcome to Puppy Parenthood!

Becoming a puppy parent is very exciting! Whether you live with others or alone, having a puppy can enrich the lives of everyone in your household. Puppies are a great way to teach children about life and responsibility – provided you know what you're doing! Right now, shelters and rescues all over the world are full of homeless dogs. Many were abandoned by families who did not fully understand what they were getting into before adopting a pet. By arming yourself with information, you can make good choices about puppy ownership and the long term commitment that is being a doting dog parent!

From left to right: Carol Fogle and puppy Dozer along with Danny Bujac, Connie Stewart and puppy Liza meet for the first time while Debbie Bollman looks on.

Chapter 1: Before the Adoption

Left to Right: Puppies Thibor and Faethor

Are You Ready for a Puppy?

Taking care of a living thing is no small matter. A new dog can be a big – and sometimes expensive – responsibility. It is best to determine if you are truly ready before taking any steps toward adoption. It is easy to say yes to big brown eyes and a wagging tail, but what about those surprise messes on the carpet or a $300 vet bill?

Your new puppy will require an initial checkup, shots and possibly deworming as well as a spay or neuter. That's if your dog is healthy when he or she arrives home. A puppy with a health condition can cost hundreds or even thousands of dollars. While this is not a common occurrence for dog owners who do their homework before adopting, it is a possibility that should be considered before bringing a puppy home.

Canines live much longer than rodents, fish and some birds. That means you must go in committed to caring for your dog for the rest of his or her life, which could be upwards of 14 to 18 years depending on breed, size and health status. If you're on the fence about puppy ownership, then ask yourself the following questions:

Do I have the financial means to afford dog food, vet care and boarding (if needed)?

Do I have the time to invest into training, play sessions and socializing?

Am I willing to make sacrifices for the health and wellbeing of my dog?

Does my living situation permit four-legged family members?

If you answered yes to all four questions, then you may be ready for a puppy! The decision is not something that should be made on a whim or even in a day. Potential dog owners should take as much time as they need to determine if puppy ownership would be a positive addition to their lives.

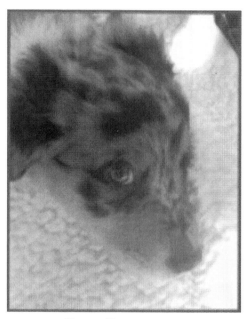

Puppy Ferno rests

Choosing a Puppy

Choosing a puppy is almost as important as making the decision to get one in the first place. Each dog breed comes with a list of strengths and potential problems. In some situations, the traits that make the breed preferred in certain arenas can make it a difficult animal to handle for some dog owners.

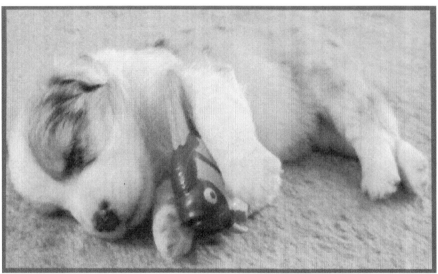
Young Thibor sleeps with a favorite toy

For example, the Border collie ranks at the top of the intelligence list. This herding breed is extremely clever, agile and athletic. In a working situation, a Border collie is superb. Take those same traits and apply them to a stationary lifestyle and the dog might develop negative behaviors. Boredom and pent up energy can lead to destroyed belongings, anxiety, non-stop barking and other issues. This doesn't mean that you have to have a huge yard to keep a Border collie happy, but it does mean you must be prepared to exercise the dog daily and engage him or her with training and play time to prevent boredom.

A Shih-Tzu, on the other hand, is less athletic and a generally calmer dog in a family situation. The breed is also smaller, which might make it more appealing in a restrictive living space. The tradeoff is that the Shih-Tzu generally requires more training and patience because it does not possess the same level of intelligence as the Border collie. If the roles were reversed, the Shih-Tzu may have a harder time keeping up with a highly athletic owner who wants a running companion.

Never choose a dog based on physical appearance. Read about the temperament, health concerns and common traits of the breeds you are interested in before making a decision. A good approach is to write down the breeds you are considering and build a list of pros and cons for each. Narrow down your options to the top two or three and go from there. Choosing a breed that complements your lifestyle can save you a lot of frustration and chewed shoes later.

Don't forget about the value of mixed breed dogs or "mutts." Mixed breed dogs can be hardier than some purebreds and are less likely to develop health conditions and behavior issues that are common with certain breeds. They are as cute, trainable and loving as any purebred dog and in many cases more accessible. They also tend to cost far less to adopt than just about any purebred dog on the planet.

Where Can I Find a Puppy?

There are many places to find a new puppy. If you want a purebred, then a breeder might be the first place you look. Dog pounds, shelters and rescues also house dogs of all ages that might be a good fit for your home. These places sometimes have purebred dogs up for adoption as well.

The internet makes it significantly easier to find available dogs in your area. Individuals and families sometimes sell or offer puppies through classified ads. Also consider expanding the distance you are willing travel to see what else is available. You may find a long term loyal companion that is well worth the extra mileage!

Nathan plays happily in his yard

Breeders

A good professional breeder will be able to answer questions with confidence and will possess a wealth of knowledge about the breed they work with as well as the lineage of each litter. They will likely have many questions for you and require a vet reference because they are invested in the long term care of their puppies. Most breeders will require an application form and/or adoption agreement to be completed and signed and will likely have specific requirements for families interested in their dogs. Breeders often cost a significant amount of money, usually in the hundreds or even thousands depending on breed. The upside is that they can provide you with your dog's family history, will be capable of answering questions and usually offer a guarantee with the adoption.

Rescues and the Humane Society

Rescues and the Humane Society often have many dogs they need to adopt out. A quick search online can help you find websites for your local rescues or Humane Society. Some rescues are breed-specific while others may not be. In many cases, the dogs are vaccinated as a requirement and may also be spayed or neutered. If not, then you may be given a discount coupon to have the procedure done after adoption. Speak with facility staff at the location you are considering to find out what is included with each adoption.

The downside is that some locations are extremely strict and may come across as unfriendly or aggressive to potential owners. You will have to complete a rather in-depth adoption form and may be asked about your home, property, and household. All family members may be required to come in and meet the new pet prior to adoption. Vet references are often required as well.

I have seen perfectly good homes turned down by the Humane Society for very minor or otherwise undisclosed reasons. It is important to remember that the individuals working for these organizations want what is best for the animal. They have seen horrible situations caused by irresponsible dog owners. It is their goal to avoid these situations and help each dog find a forever home. They want to know that you are serious, responsible and prepared to take a pet in for the rest of his or her life.

Dog Pounds

Dog pounds are different from the Humane Society and rescues. These are places that keep wayward animals that are either caught or turned in. Some locations may have lower standards in terms of cleanliness and care, which can lead to a higher risk of illness and parasites.

(Right: Young Tiberius, shortly after
his adoption from a dog pound)

That doesn't mean you cannot find
a healthy puppy at the pound. When
looking into this type of location,
make sure you have your dog
checked out by a vet as soon as
possible and be prepared to pay for
heartworm and parasite
preventatives just in case.

These locations generally do not spay or neuter the animals,
either. When adopting from a pound, make sure you add the
price of this procedure to the total cost if it is not included.

Adopting From Homes

Regular people sometimes offer puppies through classified
advertisements or word of mouth. These could be accidental
or planned litters. Accidents will happen, which is why it is
best to have pets spayed or neutered as soon as possible.
Some pet owners love their dogs so much that they want to
breed them so they can keep a puppy from the litter. Others
actually breed puppies out of their homes as a way to make
money.

These living situations may vary for the individual puppy. It
is best to ask for vet information and documentation if the
current owner claims that the puppy is up to date (UTD) on
his or her shots and has seen a vet. Don't be afraid to ask to
visit the litter and parents on site. This will also give you a
better feel for how clean and well cared for the animals are.

When adopting from a stranger, you may not have the same guarantees as you would get with a professional breeder. The process will likely be far less involved and in many cases no application form is required. This is usually the most relaxed and easiest way to adopt because you have fewer hoops to jump through, but you are also at risk if the litter was not properly cared for during the first few weeks of life.

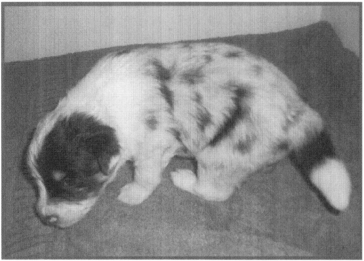
Puppy Phantom posing for the camera

A Word on Backyard Breeders

The term "Backyard Breeders" appears again and again on pet-related forums, Craig's List and elsewhere. It is important to understand what a backyard breeder really is. An accidental or one planned litter doesn't necessarily make someone a backyard breeder. The term refers to individuals who try to breed dogs at home as a way to make money, regardless of the health condition or quality of the animals being bred.

A professional breeder strives to produce high quality, healthy dogs that are excellent examples of the breed. This process requires carefully selecting males and females that will produce healthy offspring. Backyard breeders, on the other hand, are much more likely to breed puppies that have health conditions or deformities. In some cases the living conditions may also be questionable because the animals are viewed as income rather than living, breathing and loving creatures.

Never be afraid to ask questions before adopting a dog. If the breeder or owner gives you an "off" feeling, then walk away. Also keep in mind that just because someone has bred dogs at their home doesn't mean they fall into this category. Many excellent breeders handle all their litters at home because it is a big part of their lives and they are fully invested in it. The difference comes down to knowledge, living conditions and breed standards.

Chapter 2: Getting Ready for Puppy

Puppy Phantom resting under her mother's paw

Prepping Your Home

Puppies are not much different from toddlers. They are interested in their environment and will explore it once they feel comfortable. Your house may be full of puppy hazards that you didn't even know existed. It is best to address as many of these as you can before bringing your new pet home. This will also free up your time and attention so you can focus on your new furry companion as his or her first steps are taken as an official member of the family.

Start by scouting the floor level of your home. Anywhere puppy will be able to pad around should be carefully explored. Your dog will spend a lot of time at floor level, even if he or she is permitted on the furniture.

Look for stray plugs, children's toys and anything puppy can grab. Closely inspect puppy-level shelves that contain items that could attract your dog's attention. These items should be moved up and out of puppy's reach. If puppy can reach it, rest assured that he or she will eventually find it!

Power cords are a very big concern. Tuck all power cords behind furniture where puppy can't get to them. It can also help to buy or make ties that allow you to wind up excess cord and secure it so it won't unravel. Whether they are plugged in or not, electrical cords can be very dangerous for curious puppies.

Draperies and coat racks can also pose a threat, although usually a less dire one. Look out for any curtains, wall decorations or coat racks that reach the floor. A free standing coat rack can be easily pulled on its side if puppy can bite down on the end of a jacket.

Try to keep hanging objects as high up as you can. If securing them is not a possibility, then pay close attention when puppy is around. Moving large objects in front of low hanging material can also prevent puppy teeth from tearing or pulling things down.

Keep all floor-level cupboards closed as well, especially those that store household chemicals. Also make sure all heating vents and other openings near the floor are covered so puppy can't find a way inside. Taking these common sense precautions can create a healthy, happy environment for your puppy. It will also be easier on puppy parents who have to keep furry little paws and teeth out of danger!

Basic Supplies for Puppy

There are a few basic items your pup will always need. Your new dog shopping list should include a food bowl, water bowl, collar and leash. Toys are also a good idea to keep puppy from turning your favorite slippers into a plaything. One or two toys are usually sufficient, but a few more won't hurt. Buy toys based on your budget. It is better to spend more money on vet care and must-have necessities than on toys, clothing and other canine luxury items.

Dog Toy Safety Recommendations		
New Dog Toys	**Used Dog Toys**	**Other Toys**
Only buy toys recommended for your pup's size	Check all toys regularly for damage and wear	Never let puppy play with non-toy objects, such as plastic water bottles
Avoid toys that can be splintered or ripped apart in puppy confinement areas	Immediately remove any worn or damaged toys from puppy play areas	Stuffed toys are OK as long as all buttons and hard pieces have been removed
Never let puppy eat a non-edible toy	Check toys more frequently as puppy grows because his or her strength and chewing ability will increase	Cat toys or toys for other animals and children should be kept out of puppy's reach
Check toy reviews to find high quality playthings		

An old towel or blanket can serve as bedding for your puppy and may be preferable until he or she is fully housebroken. It is much easier to throw towels or a blanket in the wash than it is to scrub an expensive dog bed or padded crate liner.

Dog food is also a must-have item that will become an ongoing expense in your household. Remember to buy age-appropriate food for your puppy. The cheapest food is usually not the best for your pet. Websites can provide valuable information and reviews for current dry and wet dog foods. If you work with a breeder, ask for recommendations and find out what your puppy is currently eating. It is best to buy at least a small quantity of your dog's current food so you can ease him or her into whatever brand you select without an upset stomach. Choose a food that fits into your budget but offers your dog the highest nutritional value possible.

Grain-free foods are usually the best and generally must be purchased at pet stores or feed stores. Discount stores usually have low grade food which is not recommended and have been the focus of a number of recalls in recent years. Good dog foods cost more, but you also get more out of them. Keeping your pet on a healthy diet means he or she will be less likely to experience health problems later in life. If you spend a little more now you may save a lot on vet bills later.

To Confine or Not to Confine?

Dog confinement is a debate among some dog owners. One side of the argument believes that placing a dog in a crate or gated room is cruel. Others feel that this approach can keep the dog safe and protected. Personal experience has taught me that the crate can be a tremendous life saver that keeps my dogs happy, comfortable and calm.

(Right: Puppy Bindi rests while confined with her littermates)

You will not be able to watch your dog 24 hours a day, especially after the first day or so after the adoption. A crate provides puppy with a safe space that lets him or her relax and rest. You know your dog is secure because nothing dangerous is lurking in the crate. As long as you frequently check for items in and around the crate, it will remain a safe place. Also check for any damage caused by puppy scratching or biting the crate walls and door. Most dogs come to love their crate and view it as their "room" much like a child views his or her bedroom.

The crate should only be used when you are away, at night, during nap times or when you cannot keep an eye on your pet. As your puppy grows and matures, it may be possible to leave the crate door open all the time or get rid of it completely. Some dogs will even choose to go in the crate voluntarily to sleep or relax when they get older.

Confinement can be extremely helpful when housebreaking as well. By nature, dogs try to avoid soiling their sleeping area. Once your dog recognizes the crate as his or her personal space, it will stay relatively clean. As long as you take your puppy out for a potty break before and after crate time, you can reinforce proper potty etiquette. Also remember to buy a crate that is the right size. One that's too small will be uncomfortable but one that is too big may encourage puppy to go potty in one end and sleep in the other.

Not all dogs take well to confinement at first. Your puppy may cry until he or she adjusts. This is a normal part of the training process. Try to exercise your puppy vigorously before placing him or her in the crate. This will tire the pup out and make a nice nap much more appealing during crate time.

Avoid letting your dog out of the crate as soon as he or she starts whining. This will tell your dog that by making noises, he or she can achieve a desired effect. As the alpha member of your dog's pack, you should be the one to decide when it is time to leave the crate. It is ok to check on your dog if he or she is making noise, but don't give in if nothing is wrong.

Your pup cannot stay in the crate for extended periods of time. If your dog is frequently soiling the crate, then this could be a sign that he or she is being kept confined without a potty break for too long.

A good rule of thumb to use is to count your puppy's age in months and add one. This is the total number of hours your dog can comfortably stay in the crate. For example, a one month old puppy shouldn't be in a crate without a potty break for more than two hours. A four month old puppy can go five hours.

Dogs are not nocturnal, so your puppy should be able to stay in the crate longer for bedtime. Young puppies may need a break in the middle of the night. It is best to plan for this by letting your puppy out halfway through the evening so you aren't stuck cleaning up an unpleasant mess in the early morning hours. Schedule your puppy's evening outings based on your sleep schedule.

Puppy Blaze sleeps on a blanket

If you go to bed earlier, then your pup may need an earlier evening break or two. This should only be done during the early housetraining phase. You should not continue to do this as the puppy grows unless you want the midnight potty break to become a regular thing when the puppy is an adult.

Work towards setting your dog on a schedule that is comfortable for him or her and is compatible with your daily routine.

Young Nathan nips a pillow

Who Will Care for Puppy?

It is vital to know who will be responsible for puppy's daily care. Unless you live alone, this is an issue that should be addressed with all members of your household. Adults will likely have work schedules and should be aware of when they will be expected to pick up puppy duty. Communication is a must because if someone misses their assigned puppy time, your new furry friend will be the one to suffer for it. If more than one person will be responsible for the dog then consider creating a daily chart or calendar. Everyone should be held accountable to ensure that puppy is properly cared for every day.

Connie Stewart with her new puppy, Liza

There is no 'right' way to determine who will care for the new family pet. The best way to approach the issue is to sit down with all family members who will be included in the puppy care schedule and discuss it. Find out who will be available when and work as a team to make sure no feedings or potty breaks are missed. Some individuals take on the whole responsibility themselves while others split it between parents or the adults and older children in the household. Design a shared schedule that works for your family's living situation with your dog's health and best interests in mind.

Puppy Baeli poses for a photo

Puppy Responsibilities and Children

Baby Gavin plays with Puppy Blaze

Parents must be very careful when handing off puppy duty to their children. Very young children should not be expected to care for a puppy on their own. A dog is not the same as a goldfish. The dog needs someone who can walk, feed and take proper care of him or her. Parents can still teach young children about animal care and responsibilities by allowing them to care for puppy with mom or dad as helpers.

I have seen instances where adults adopt a dog "for the kids." When the kids lose interest and stop taking care of the family pet, the parents dump the dog off at the pound or elsewhere. Adults in the household must keep in mind that no matter what children of any age say – whether they are 7 or 17 – the adults should be willing to take care of the pet. If the adult has no interest, then a dog is not the right pet for the household. Getting a dog and getting rid of it is bad for the animal and may reduce the value of life in the eyes of the children in the household. It can reinforce the idea that when something requires work they should get rid of it.

Some children and teenagers are very responsible and this may never be an issue in your household. I include this section in because I have seen it happen and I hope to prevent it in the future. It's a sad situation for all involved. Parents should never get a dog "for the kids." A dog should be adopted "for the family."

New born puppy, Liza

That means the adults in the household are willing to take on 100% of the responsibility for the dog's entire lifetime should the children not live up to their end of the bargain. It is also possible that older children and teenagers may end up going to college or moving out in the dog's lifetime, which is another situation that will require the adults to take over all dog duties.

If you are willing to be a dog parent regardless of whether other family members in your household will help, then you are ready to go out and get your dream puppy!

Puppy Nathan responds eagerly to "sit"

Chapter 3: Puppy Arrives Home

Left to Right: Liza and Phantom on adoption day

Puppy's First Hour

Your first hour with puppy will be an exciting one! Get things started on the right paw by introducing puppy to his or her potty area before going into your home for the first time. Be patient and allow puppy several minutes to sniff and explore the area. This helps familiarize your new dog with a spot that he or she will come to know well and gives the pup a chance to go if needed. Avoid ushering the pup in too quickly or you may wind up with your first puppy mess on the carpet!

Going Inside

Slowly introduce your new pet to his or her living space. Don't expect your puppy to go romping right away – although some do! Each puppy is an individual and may react differently to different situations. The last thing you want to do is terrify the pup when showing him or her around. Find a nice, open spot in your home where puppy will be permitted to explore.

Dozer waits to go home on adoption day

If other adults or children are in your home as well, make sure they stay calm and relaxed. Loud noises can scare puppies and some may become skittish if they are being crowded. Others are more curious and will explore openly. Make sure you call your puppy using his or her new name, even if the pup doesn't seem to understand. Eventually they will catch on!

As your pup grows comfortable, calmly introduce him or her to each member of the household. This should include other animals that may come in contact with the puppy. Your pet fish really doesn't need to be introduced, but the family cat should be if he or she will be sharing the same living space. Remember to keep the environment as relaxed and inviting as possible. Use lowered voices and avoid yelling, screaming or loud laughter.

Keep a close eye on your pup in case he or she shows signs of needing to go to the designated potty area. If you suddenly notice excessive floor sniffing, then the pup may be looking for a place to go. If the pup begins squatting or crouching, pick him or her up calmly and head to the potty area as quickly as possible. The faster you are at identifying these cues and getting the puppy outside, the more success your pup will have with housebreaking at a young age.

Dragon relaxing at home

Puppy's First 24 Hours

The first full day with puppy should be a positive experience for all involved. Try to maintain the same calm environment as you did during the first hour. As puppy gets acquainted, he or she will be better able to handle the various situations and experiences your home has to offer. This should be viewed as a time for puppy to adjust. Begin working on a regular schedule, but don't push too hard. Your pup will have to go potty on his or her own time however you can control that to some extent by planning each feeding throughout the day. The pup will likely have to go within an hour or two of eating, so feed your pup with that in mind.

Do not leave food down for puppy all the time. This is a good way to grow your pup into an obese dog. It also doesn't help you monitor overall canine health and habits. If you know how much and when your dog eats, you can quickly identify a serious health condition if he or she suddenly stops eating or eats less.

If you are having trouble getting puppy to eat, try feeding inside the crate where there are fewer distractions. Older puppies can be given a time limit until they learn to finish their meal when it is provided rather than when they feel like it. Taking food away during a feeding or two if your pup is lingering can teach a valuable lesson without harming the dog.

Puppy's First Week

Some new pet owners choose to take time off work and other commitments to care for puppy during the first few days at home. This is a great idea, as long as you plan for the long term as well. A very young puppy will need to go out more frequently. If you work a regular eight hour a day job, make sure you have a plan in place to get puppy out of the crate or confined area. This could include enlisting the help of a friend or family member to take puppy out throughout the day or stopping home during lunch hour. Eventually your puppy will be able to wait until after work (unless you work an extremely long shift), but early on this is vital to forming good potty habits. The fewer indoor accidents your dog has, the better!

Devote time each day to puppy, aside from potty breaks and feedings. This should include playing and letting puppy get to know you. You can start reinforcing basic commands, such as your pup's name, but don't expect your pup to become the next Lassie at such a young age. Unless your dog is a prodigy, he or she will need time and effort to learn advanced obedience commands.

General Recommended Training Progression

6 to 8 Weeks

Introduce puppy to the leash with short walks at home

Begin working on basic commands, including "sit" and "lay down"

Do not confine for more than two to three hours at a time

Under 3 Months

Practice basic commands

Introduce a few advanced commands

Monitor individual progress and increase or reduce command complexity if needed

Do not confine for more than three to four hours at a time

Over 3 Months

Gradually increase training session duration

Avoid exceeding 15 minutes per session

Use the age in month's plus one hour rule for confinement without exceeding 7 to 8 hours for adult dogs

You should see improvements in your pup's housebreaking. Pay close attention to your dog's potty cues. You may notice that he or she looks at the door that you usually use to go to the designated relief area when it is time. If you see any movement in that direction, take the pup out immediately. This is progress! Some dogs don't make a sound, but only look or move a few steps towards the door when they need to go. Others will jump and scratch and make a production out of it. Either way, make sure you catch it and react quickly to reinforce the good behavior your dog is displaying. Always have the leash or anything else you need for potty breaks within reach of the door because timing is very important!

Nathan cools in the shade

Dog Grooming at Home

Dog grooming supplies are not required for the first few days, but they are recommended necessities. Even if you plan on taking your dog to a professional groomer, you should still be equipped to take care of minor grooming needs at home. Some elements of grooming are vital to a healthy and comfortable life for your pet. A dog brush and nail clippers are the absolute minimum every pet owner should have on hand. It is best to review your dog's breed to determine which specialized grooming tools will be necessary.

During your puppy's first week, begin a regular routine of brushing and gentle nail clipping. You do not have to go all out with a bath and extensive trims. It is unlikely your pup will have hair and nails long enough to require a serious grooming yet. Do this to introduce your dog to the typical actions associated with grooming.

An adult dog that is not accustomed to grooming may react poorly and become a handful. Even an otherwise well behaved dog may become afraid when his or her nails or fur are trimmed. Some dogs take better to grooming than others. By starting early and at home, you can familiarize your dog with the process, even if you aren't fully grooming them. Taking a nearly invisible snip of nail or fur will help your dog relax and become accustomed to grooming, no matter who is actually doing it.

Prior to grooming, make sure you review the proper procedure for your dog's breed as well as the correct way to trim nails. Some fur types have specific needs while others are nearly maintenance-free. A tangled mess that is not taken care of can cause long fur to pull the skin and leave behind painful welts. A comfortable dog is one that is properly groomed on a regular basis. This process also helps reduce dog odors and allows you to check for abnormalities on the skin as well as parasites like fleas and ticks. A daily outdoor brushing can significantly reduce the amount of pet fur that winds up on your carpets and furniture and it gives you another way to bond with your pet.

Socializing Puppy

Once puppy has seen a vet and been given shots and a clean bill of health, consider taking walks in your neighborhood. If you know anyone with a puppy-friendly dog, you may want to introduce your new companion. The earlier you begin socializing the better your dog will be with others when he or she grows up. Remember to try socializing in different environments with humans, canines and other animals. Let your puppy meet children and adults as well as cats and dogs. A little playtime each day can go a long way in puppy's social development!

Young Nathan and Puppy Caladesi socialize

When socializing, it is important to remember that you are responsible for your dog's wellbeing and safety. Not all children know how to handle a small pup and not all dogs are friendly towards playful puppies. Avoid putting your puppy in overwhelming situations, such as a group of dogs at a dog park or a group of unruly children at the playground. Stay in control and observe all interactions so you can stop any potentially harmful behavior. A small child may pet puppy too hard or an adolescent dog may try to play rough. This can physically hurt your dog.

Even if your dog is not physically hurt, this type of event can make him or her fearful and may have a negative impact on behavior later in life. Instruct children to be gentle and keep puppy in your sight at all times when socializing. When meeting other dogs, it is best to keep them and puppy on leash so they can be separated if things get too intense. Stay in control and be prepared to keep puppy safe. It is your responsibility as a dog owner and your pet will thank you for it later with great social skills!

Sean Bollman and puppy Nathan enjoy a swim

Chapter 4: A Long and Happy Life with Puppy

Nathan relaxes after a round of fetch

Bonding with Puppy

A good dog owner will want to form a lasting bond with their pet. The relationship between human and canine can be an amazing thing. You and your dog can begin building a strong bond as soon as your pup arrives home. Try working on basic training, which helps establish your role in your pet's life. Good starter commands include a basic recall (your dog responding to his or her name), sit, lay and stay. Sit should be learned first, after the recall, because it is among the easiest for your pet to understand. It is also much easier to teach "lay" and "stay" if your dog already knows "sit."

There are different training options available. The clicker method can be very effective as well as inexpensive. If you choose a method that includes rewarding with treats, avoid over-treating your dog. Too many treats can cause your dog to expect to be fed each time he or she responds to a command. If you stop giving out treats, your pet may be less inclined to obey. Good old fashioned praise can work wonders to reward and motivate your dog. The occasional treat reward for big steps in the right direction with plenty of positive praise is a good way to go.

Young puppies will have shorter attention spans, so plan for short training sessions. These often work better with adult dogs as well. Once your dog loses interest, it will become nearly impossible to teach him or her anything. A few minutes here or there and up to 10 or 15 minutes when he or she is older is often sufficient. If your dog seems frustrated take a step back and work on commands he or she knows then slowly introduce a new command. Always praise your pet, even when performing familiar commands. Just like humans, dogs can lose motivation if they do not receive positive reinforcement.

Plan to exercise your puppy regularly with play sessions and walks as well. These activities keep your pup healthy, burn off excess energy and allow you to bond. Walking the dog may sound a bit stereotypical of dog owners but is a very good activity for bonding. Teach your dog the "heel" command and lead him or her on walks. This type of leadership helps establish your position as the alpha member of your dog's pack.

Owner Allan Gatto and Caladesi play at North Park

Exercise and training are two of the best ways to bond with your furry friend. Early on there may be many obstacles as your pup learns how to behave and you learn how to train and guide a pet. Bringing your dog along on family trips, visits and other situations that are canine-friendly will also have a positive impact on your relationship. Just remember to ask before bringing your pet to another person's home or event!

As you both grow and mature as dog and owner, you will see a beautiful bond forming that strengthens with each exercise and training session.

Adult Tiberius leaps for a tennis ball

A Lifetime of Love

A new puppy is a big commitment that can offer big rewards. If you take the time to find the perfect dog and invest the energy, effort and money necessary you can have a companion for many, many years. Canines can have a profound impact on the lives they touch. The dog is willing to give his all for us. It only seems fair that we do all we can to give our canine companions the best life possible from day one. Taking the responsibility seriously and making the proper preparations can keep your first days together as pleasant as possible. Good luck to you and your new dog!

Adult Tiberius plays in his yard

Suggested Web Resources

The following websites can help you learn more about canine care:

The American Kennel Club
www.AKC.org

The official American Kennel Club website provides a wealth of information on canines as well as recognized breed profiles.

ASPCA
www.ASPCA.org

The American Society for the Prevent of Cruelty to Animals (ASPCA) is an organization that helps prevent, stop and raise awareness of animal cruelty. The ASPCA also provides information on pet care related issues.

Dog Food Analysis
www.DogFoodAnalysis.com

The Dog Food Analysis website provides users with a searchable database of dog foods. Users can find reviews, detailed nutrition information and a rating system that makes selecting a high quality food much easier.

The Humane Society
www.HumaneSociety.org

This is the official website of the Human Society of the United States. Visitors can find information on pet care, pet-related news stories and more. Many local Human Societies also maintain individual websites that may include available pet profiles.

PetFinder
www.PetFinder.com

PetFinder is an online search that lets users find pets in the United States. The site has an extensive collection of pets, most of which are listed from shelters, rescues and pounds. Users can browse by location and filter results by breed, age, animal type and group.

RSPCA
www.RSPCA.org.uk

This is the official Royal Society for the Prevention of Cruelty to Animals (RSPCA) website. The RSPCA is a United Kingdom-based organization focused on the welfare of animals. Much like the ASPCA website, the RSPCA site provides helpful information, tips and pet-related stories.

About the Author

Shel Gatto resides in western Pennsylvania with her four- and two-legged family members. She has extensive personal experience with canines, which have been a part of her life since she was a child. Shel's love of writing and man's best friend were the basis for the creation of this guide. The images included feature her beloved dogs, their puppies and the caring families who adopted them.